香港國際詩歌之夜 2013
INTERNATIONAL POETRY NIGHTS IN HONG KONG

編輯 Editors

北島 Bei Dao

陳嘉恩 Shelby K. Y. Chan

方梓勳 Gilbert C. F. Fong

柯夏智 Lucas Klein

馬德松 Christopher Mattison

洛楓
Natalia S. H. Chan

目錄 Contents

1 走過除夕與元旦的交界2003

將歲月披在身上
讓它的衣袖比手臂長
將衣裳留在歲月裡
讓它的容顏比潮流恆久

入冬以後
溫度計時刻反臉無常
冷縮熱脹的心情
隨著聖誕的歌聲浮浮沉沉
把日曆紙翻到盡頭
撕下舊賬是否真的可以新年進步？
除夕之前患癌病的歌手
趕上她最後的旅程
原來「從頭開始」的時節
是這樣令人措手不及

把空調昇到第八音節的購物中心
讓隱形的空氣凝結可見的冰天雪地
人造的雪景和會搖頭的北極熊
告訴沉溺死亡的城市再生的可能
商場的中央從某天開始

矗立了一座四層高的聖誕樹
塑膠或絲絹的綠松葉
配襯會發亮閃光的白水晶
樹上高高掛著贊助商的名字
以及天鵝剪影的白色商標
抬頭仰視射燈下縱橫錯亂的枝葉與閃光
她從此相信
自己也是一隻天鵝
早已脱離醜小鴨的磨難
渴望飛　但燈光的幻影使她沉淪不起
直到樓梯盡頭

走過重重疊疊的自動升降機
從底層開始
每一步都是上昇
仰望頂樓玻璃的天幕
星星、月亮和太陽彷彿垂手可得
但走近了才知道
原來那是激光投映的圖案
遠處傳來雄壯愉悦的歌詠和聖詩
面前只有兩手空空抱住一件oversize的大衣

原來新年的祝願可以如此飽滿和輕盈
輕得如昇空的汽球或月球
樓梯的彎角有風
在來年與去年之間
她重新披上大衣
讓歲月比衣裳薄
衣裳比歲月長

Crossing over from New Year's Eve to New Year's Day, 2003

Drape the years over your body
may its sleeves be longer than your arms
leave your clothes inside the years to come
may its look last longer than the fashion

Since the start of winter
the thermometer constantly changes its face
people's moods fluctuate
with the highs and lows of Christmas carols
turn the calendar to its last page
does tearing up old debts really bring in the new year?
On New Year's Eve a singer with cancer
ends her last trip
so in this season of "new beginnings"
we're taken off-guard

The shopping mall has its air on the highest octave
and the invisible air crystalizes into scenes of snow and
 ice
the polar bears shake their heads at the manmade snow

and tell the dead city about the possibility of renewal
then one day in the middle of the mall
a four-story tall Christmas tree springs up
its green plastic or silk pine needles
flash with sparkling white crystals
the names of sponsors hang high on the tree
with paper cutouts of a white swan trademark
as she looks up at the branches twinkling under
    spotlights
she believes
she's also a swan
who has long escaped an ugly duckling's fate
she longs to fly   but the flashing lights weigh her
    down
straight to the top of the stairs

Walking up escalator after escalator
starting from the lowest floor
with each step
she looks up at the glass roof

where the stars and moon and sun all seem within
  reach
only to realize when she gets close
that they are only laser projections
from some distant place come happy songs and carols
she holds an oversized coat in both hands
full and light like New Year's wishes
light as a bubble or a moon rising in the sky
wind blows past the bend in the staircase
between last year and the new one
she puts on her coat again
may the years be thinner than her clothes
may her clothes be longer than the years

(Translated by Eleanor Goodman)

2 自我紙盒藏屍的日子

患病的身體捲曲、怕光
畏懼聲音　然而喜歡潮濕
這是一段自我紙盒藏屍的日子
我用收縮的瞳孔
擴張四面紙壁的闊度
看見自己腐化的心逐漸變硬
而且晶瑩透亮

在熬過二百四十四天後
我從紙盒爬出　在嚴寒的低溫搭上
有空調的長途巴士　（如同另一個鐵盒）
從光天白日走到烏天黑地
這城市有人、有燈
車子走在半空　從天橋望入樓房
晃動的人影　電視藍色的聲浪
悠揚播送飯香
轉入直路車輪差點碰撞行人的腳跟
紅紅綠綠的減價招牌
跟熒光屏上的廣告歌曲互相吆喝
我想　聖誕節也快來臨了
然後是新年　元宵　情人節

清明和復活節　週而復始
怎麼辦呢這麼連綿無盡的節日氣氛？

走得累了是這一雙滿佈紅絲的眼睛
有閃光的暈眩　無法分辨
城市密集的燈影和人群
幸福的節日祝禱馬上就要開始
怎麼辦呢這麼繁盛的喧囂？
父母帶著孩子上車下車
情侶挽著手臂從車頭走到車尾
只有老人走得最慢最不被原諒
怎麼辦呢這麼容易被擠跌的空間？

終於車子也駛過你當日
從高空躍下的酒店門口
撞毀的鐵欄已經修補　血跡和鮮花
都已成新聞圖片　這城市
總有新的燈飾替換每日的故事
從車窗隔著玻璃望向逐漸收窄的港灣
我們有理由相信　明年今日
是必須延續下去的！

在不能忍受新陳代謝與新舊交替的情況下
最後我還是決定再過一段
自我紙盒藏屍的日子
戒掉水、希望和光
好好跟自己相處

Days When I Hide My Corpse in a Cardboard Box

This sick body curls up, fears the light
dreads sound   but likes the damp
these are the days I hide my corpse in a cardboard box
I see through contracted pupils
the expanded width of the four paper walls
my rotting heart hardens bit by bit
turning glittering and transparent

After enduring two hundred forty-four days
I climb out of the box   and in the hypothermic
   cold
take a cool long distance bus (another steel box)
from bright daylight to the black night
in the city there are people and streetlamps,
cars drive through midair   looking into buildings
   from the overpass
the swaying shadows of people   blue clamor of
   televisions
the far-wafting scent of cooking
turning, the bus wheels almost hit the pedestrians'

heels
red and green sales signs
and fluorescent advertising jingles shout at each other
I think   Christmas must be coming
and then it's New Year   Lantern Festival
Valentine's Day
Grave-Sweeping Day and Easter   year after year
after year
how do we deal with these continuous interminable
holidays?

What's tired now are these bloodshot eyes
dizzy from the flashes   unable to distinguish
the city's dense lights and crowds
the holiday well-wishing is about to begin
how do we deal with all the commotion?
Parents take their children on and off the bus
lovers go arm in arm from the front of the bus to the
back
the slow-moving elderly are least likely to be forgiven

how do we deal with such a packed jostling space?

Finally the bus drives past the entrance
of the hotel from whose heights you leapt that day
the shattered steel fence has been repaired   the
    blood stains and flowers
are just pictures in the news   in this city
there are always new lights switching stories every day
looking out through the window at the gradually
    narrowing harbor
we have reason to believe   that next year
will still go on!

I can't stand all this change from old to new
so in the end I decide to spend more time
hiding my corpse in a cardboard box
I give up water, hope, and light
to spend some more time with myself

(Translated by Eleanor Goodman)

3 飛天棺材

凌晨五時被雷聲劈醒
醒來第一句想跟你說的話
是我們的算計都錯誤了

房子外面有一條公路
公路上有一種飛天棺材
棺材內的十六條性命
只交給一個司機
如果他不喝酒、不抽煙、不談手提電話
如果天不下雨、不長霧
路邊不閃出小狗或老人
我相信是可以長命富貴的
常常在亡命的旅途上
聽同一首歌哼重覆的拍子
每次歌詞昇到最高的音節時
車子總剛巧滑過一個死亡的彎角
車輪傳來撕裂的呼喊
拋出愛情的離心力使人虛脫
於是便記起凌晨五時雷聲的警號
我們真的無路可走嗎？

假日的時候公路總堵滿車子
像無頭無尾的彩色蜈蚣
彎彎曲曲的關節兩頭都不是結局或開始
沿路有警察維持或干預秩序
卻無法改善寸步難移的局面
當路途因外來的擠壓而變得踟躕的時候
是不是該放棄原地踏步呢？
當後面的車子不耐煩地碰撞前面的時候
是不是該設法逃離現場呢？
鐳射唱片的音樂依舊流動
沒有因天氣、距離或交通事故而停頓
然而
愛冒險的小巴司機突然也會心血來潮
在危急關頭考驗闖過黃燈的速度
剎時撞向石壆再反彈鐵欄
才發現連唱盤也會跳針電源也會中斷
原來相愛很難
當你在公路的那頭我在這頭的時候

沿路有什麼風景　我們
便只可選擇怎樣的窗口

從天橋到地面
從來都不是一個踏實的轉向
我們以為平放地上的
會比懸盪空中的易於掌握
卻不知道半空的視線才可
鳥瞰路面的全景
只是風景的切換太快
在來不及記認每個細節之前
你已經在相反的車線上跟我再見

凌晨五時從黑洞醒來才記起
我們的愛情
是開在公路上的飛天棺材
隨時會死在半途上

21.6.2002

The Flying Coffin

Woken by thunder at five in the morning
the first thing I want to tell you
is that all our plans have gone wrong

Outside our building is a highway
on the highway is a flying coffin
inside the coffin are sixteen lives
all handed over to the driver
if he doesn't drink or smoke or talk on his cell phone
if it doesn't rain or turn foggy
if no dogs or old people suddenly appear in the road
I believe we will lead long full lives
often on these desperate escapes
I listen to the same song and hum along
each time the song rises to its highest pitch
the minibus swerves by a deadly corner
the wheels squeal
and everyone collapses in the centrifugal force of lost love
and so I remember the thunder's warning before dawn
do we really have no way forward?

On holidays the highway is one big traffic jam
like a colorful centipede with neither head nor tail
the zigzagging links at either extreme are neither the
beginning nor end
along the way the police preserve or disturb order
but there's no improving an impossible situation
when pressure builds into indecision
should we abandon the gridlock?
When a car hits the one in front
should it try to flee the scene?
The CD's music keeps flowing
not even pausing for the weather or distance or accident
even so
the reckless driver of the minibus is suddenly seized by a
whim
to speed through a yellow light at a critical juncture
and in an instant it collides with the curb and bounces
back to the railing
with the skip of the disc and cut power I realize
it's truly hard to love each other
when you're at one end of the highway and I'm at the other

What we see along the way
is determined by which window we choose
from the overpasses to the roads
there's never been a right way to turn
we thought being on the ground
would be easier than being suspended in the sky
but didn't realize that only in midair
would we get a full bird's-eye view
it's just that the scene changed so fast
that before there was a chance to remember each detail
you were saying goodbye from the opposite lane

Only waking from the abyss of five o'clock did I remember
that our love
is a flying coffin speeding down the highway
and at any moment it can hit a dead end

(Translated by Eleanor Goodman)

4 一舞入魂

拐著高跟鞋來追風你的舞步
握著單程的票走迴旋的樓梯
被鎖住的凝望猶如兜轉的裙襬
踏亂了呼吸的次序
室內無風但我的思慮有一個黑洞
攪動的碎石如冰
哐啷哐啷的碰撞帶著透明的清脆
不能言說的一句話即將道破
如何才可免於落地對你的驚擾？
只好將迷戀與迷亂擊成粉末　再散入
嘈嘈切切錯彈的視線

布幕拉起時你橫向的背立在
橢圓的燈區
閃著暈眩的紙屑從頂端灑落
如斷線的緣份極力抓住急降的飄離
墜落原是為了串連啊
如何才可免於命運的崩解？
旋起的氣流像纏繞的線
來自你曾經抱住的臂彎給我緊張的力度
琴音滑過鬆脫的空隙

你甩開拘禁的慾望讓四肢大開大合
翻成地上枝葉蔓延的動作
在沒有人愛沒有人的瓜葛裏
讓藤纏著瓜瓜纏著花

灰色的佈景不斷變換迷陣
走過起伏的線條你的身體
從這扇門隱沒那扇窗
從來無法分清左右
當你在台上我在台下的時候
不是鏡與影的依存
卻假想你在台上看得見
我在台下看著你在台上
彷彿只有這種迂迴
我們才能如此親近

當影子疊著影子的時候
我們便跌入雙重黑暗
你在台上四面遊走尋找光源
我依舊被命定於觀眾席上

繼續曖昧不明
然後燈滅無聲
你的身影倏忽消失剎那帶來驚恐
會不會就這樣從此不見？
驟然你的舞影似箭
射入黑暗的盡頭
我便看見了光

當燈再亮時你原來仍在那裏
汗濕的背站在方形的燈區
守住一個等待的姿勢如銅牆鐵壁
不容眼神洞穿
也不允許掌聲擊潰
就這樣我和你對峙
直到騷動的人群靜止——

1.3.2012

Spirit Dance

Turning in high heels to find your dancing
I grasp my one-way ticket up the spiral staircase
my locked stare is like a spinning skirt
trampling the sequence of my breath
the room is airless but a black hole sits in my thoughts
where gravel churns up like ice
the little collisions bringing a transparent sharpness
what cannot be spoken is about to be revealed
how can I keep my landing from disturbing you?
Best to crush attraction and confusion   and scatter
 them
into the misplayed sightlines.

When the curtain opens you have your back
to the oval spotlight
bright confetti sprinkles down from above
like broken fate trying to catch what floats there
such falling is supposed to connect things
now how can it avoid disintegration?
The whirling air is like the tangled threads
of the nervous strength the curve of your arms once
 gave me

sound glides through the loosening gap
you lose the imprisonment of desire and let your limbs
open and close
they turn into the spreading of leaves and branches
and in lovelessness and disassociation
vines entangle the melons and melons entangle the
flowers

The gray scenery keeps changing its maze
of undulating lines and your body
disappears from this door to that window
always indistinct
when you're onstage and I'm in the audience
we're not like some co-dependent mirror and image
yet suppose that onstage you're watching
me in the audience watching you onstage
it seems that only in this cycle
can we get close

When shadows pile on shadows
we fall into double darkness

you walk across the stage seeking the source of light
I'm destined to stay in the audience
to be obscure
then the lights go out and the music stops
your sudden disappearance is shocking
will you ever be seen again?
Suddenly your dancing shadow shoots out like an
  arrow
to the ends of the darkness
and I can see the light

When the lights come up again you're still there
back wet with sweat and standing in a square of light
waiting like a fortress
letting no gazes penetrate   letting no applause affect
  you
so you and I face each other
until the crowd falls silent—

(Translated by Eleanor Goodman)

5 戀戀風SARS

從此你我必須相隔三呎距離
從此我要戴上口罩跟你説話
從此我們不能握手只可道別
直到我的身體對你非典型的情愛
產生免疫的抗體為止

四月的季候風慵懶、羞澀而且兇猛
帶來城市疫症的花粉並且蔓延
你電郵決絕的病毒
打開窗戶如同打開死亡的溝渠
我無法辨認站在二十四樓的高度
當摯愛的歌手用飄落的身影
糊住生命的視線
我對你原有的思念便嘭然中斷
零碎四散的雨點擊在欄杆上
原來
真的
很痛

在風和它的沙和SARS戀戀廣播的日子
小島的燈火因虛怯而浮腫和無眠

閉上眼睛我聽見
長途電話另一端你的歌聲
急促的呼吸斷續的言詞
卡在哽咽的喉鼻間便無可挽回
告訴你家中的小貓病了
我們隨時會死在隱瞞的病變裏
你說時間過了限期
敏感的城市總會積壓抑鬱的基因
無可避免無一倖免
放下話筒躺在床上直到清晨六時
閉塞的天空始終無法亮起
一個呼吸暢順的早晨
想到有一天
當我對你不再提防免疫的時候
或許我們便可除下N95的障礙
點頭、微笑、再分道揚鑣
從此、
然後——

The Loving Wind and SARS

From now on we keep three feet apart
from now on I wear a surgical mask to talk with you
from now on we can't hold hands, just say goodbye
until my body's severe, acute love for you
produces antibodies

The monsoons of April are sluggish, shy, but fierce
bringing a pestilence of pollen to the city that extends
to the virus that shut down your email
to open a window is to open up a canal of death
I don't know the height of the twenty-fourth floor
but when my beloved singer blurred life's sight
with his down-drifting body
and the longing I felt for you ended abruptly
scattered raindrops struck the railings
and as a matter of fact
it really
hurt

These days the wind and sand broadcast SARS
the island's lights are weak, swollen and sleepless

I close my eyes and hear
your singing on the other end of the long distance call
words interrupted by gasps
get caught in your throat with sobs and are lost forever
I tell you my kitten is sick
we could die anytime from some hidden illness
you say your time is up
a depressive gene overwhelms this sensitive city
unavoidable, inescapable
I hang up and lie in bed until six in the morning
the heavy sky doesn't brighten
a morning of easy breathing
I think of a day
when I'll no longer be on guard against infection
maybe we can take off our N95 barriers
and nod, smile, and part again
from now on,
and after—

(Translated by Eleanor Goodman)

6 感情幹線

Sometimes the snow comes down in June
Sometimes the sun goes 'round the moon
Sometimes 我和你分叉
城市高危吊詭的幹線

每當列車隆隆駛入月台的剎那
漆黑的隧道總會空白一片
沒有血色的玻璃門上注滿
一雙一對鬼影幢幢的眼睛
看不透門外蠕動的風景
除了努力抓緊一根金屬的扶手外
我們別無他法制止
情感迅速的滑落

無論踏入還是踏出車廂
我們都不能逃避月台的跨越
無論是追、趕、跑、跳
這一步原是無可厚非的
讓中途的路程提前圓滿
但往往只有「請勿超越黃線」

或「小心月台空隙」的警告
霸佔你我密集擠塞的思維
唯是欠缺這個姿勢
我們終於也無法行行重行行了

把最好的都留在最後
管它是月台還是舞台
毋須送我回家
也不打算眷顧你流連的背影
就讓兩邊相反相成的隧道
同時響起列車開動的噪音
那時候期待　你依然相信
Sometimes the snow comes down in June
Sometimes the sun goes 'round the moon
Sometimes 我和你分叉
兩條終極無間的感情線

16.10.2003

Tracks of Emotion

Sometimes the snow comes down in June
Sometimes the sun goes 'round the moon
Sometimes we diverge
on the city's strange and dangerous tracks

When each train roars into the station
a section of the pitch-black tunnel turns blank
the color-drained glass door fills
with pair after pair of ghostly sparkling eyes
that can't see through to the scene creeping by
aside from grasping onto the metal handles
we have no way of stopping
our emotions from quickly slipping by

No matter how we step in or out of the train
we can't avoid the platform gap
whether chasing, catching up, running, jumping
it is a blameless step
that completes a half-finished journey
but there are often warnings "Please stand behind
the yellow line"

or “mind the gap”
our thoughts are crammed with them
but we still lack the right mindset
and in the end we can’t go on or start again

Leave the best for last
whether on the platform or the stage
there’s no need to see me home
I won’t be tender toward your parting shadow
let the equal and opposite tunnels
ring with the simultaneous noises of two trains starting
  up
then with hope   you still believe
Sometimes the snow comes down in June
Sometimes the sun goes ’round the moon
Sometimes we diverge
on these two unending tracks of emotion

(Translated by Eleanor Goodman)

7 當城市蒼老的時候

當這個城市開始蒼老
我們還可以年輕多久？

回歸的晚上
到處是煙花的幻影
散落於城市每一張臉孔
浮游、明滅而零零瑣瑣
幽冷的你陪著蒼白的我走過
一段蜿長、曲折而傾斜的路
催促的車聲、沸騰的人群
喀嚓喀嚓從身邊掠過
猶如失落的煙火
把美豔的繁華都拖在背後

下過雨的台階
有幢幢濕滑的倒影
蘭桂坊的酒香
舞旋於燃著點點霓虹的星空
有柔軟的歌聲從擠擁的角落冒起
參與節目的人互相擁抱和祝福
走在你的背後

我低頭避開簷蓬的雨水
卻看見一張裝飾的布幔
飄起你單薄的身影
推開四方八面的人潮
抱著冬夜一般墨藍的沉默與寒意
我追趕你前行的腳步
輕微的雨花瀟瀟灑灑
視線罩起了一層煙霞
剎那間我竟無從確認
這城市與你
真實的輪廓

假如這城市已經衰老
我們還可以年輕多久？

午夜十二時過後
聽說是另一個時代的開始
路邊有打翻的酒瓶
碎裂的玻璃折射幽暗的綠光
我們停步、回頭
搜尋來時的風景

空空洞洞的風颳起無處歸落的髮梢
靠近你的身旁
聽醉漢的歌聲寥落一條黑漆的冷巷
熱鬧在街的另一頭響起
我們該如何走過這世紀的路程？

世紀的旅程
以節目的嘉年華開始
豔紅、輝煌而喜氣洋洋
有人穿起了民族的服飾舞動一條
還未睡醒的金龍有人拉起了咿啞的胡琴奏出
吞吞吐吐的樂章有人搭起了白色的舞台
以笨重的身軀疊起團結的圖案
但今夜你穿了疲倦的黑衣
臉上遺失了歡愉的表情是因為
不習慣璀璨的氣氛還是
太慣於靜默的表達？

聚滿人群的廣場我們走過
一座新近矗立水中的亭園
朱紅的飛簷勾起了歷史與文化

抽象的括弧
立法局大樓洶湧傳來
米高風擴大了的論辯
離開圍觀的鎂光燈我們繞著大樓
走了一個圈子
不是為了悼念即將隱沒的圓柱與拱廊
只是微雨的昏夜我們無從躲閃
翳悶混濁的空氣
我們仰視樓頂女神手持的天秤
侷促地呼吸下一個世紀的夜空
閃電藏於天的右邊
燈火與歌聲盛放於左邊
企立在曖昧的中央地帶
我只想抓緊一個實在的身影
你低頭看我
我轉頭去看八面玲瓏的燈飾
相反相成的人潮裏
我倆單薄如落在地上的雨花

雨花越織越大
道路與睡意漸漸傾斜

側著肩膊看你濃密的眉毛
問你能否讓我知道：
當我們開始蒼老
這個城市還可以年輕多久？

1.7.1997

When the City Gets Old

When this city starts to get old
how long can we stay young?

The night of the handover
apparitions of fireworks were everywhere
scattering over every face in the city
ephemeral, flickering and gone
on our walk you were cold and remote, I was wan
on the winding slanted road
the impatient cars and seething crowds
zoomed past us
like falling fireworks
dragging their extravagant beauty behind them

The rain-drenched steps
flickered with wet reflections
a smell of alcohol from Lan Kwai Fong
whirled with the points of neon in the sky
soft singing seeped out from the crowded corners
revelers embraced and wished each other well
walking behind you

I lowered my head to avoid the rain from the canopies
and watched your patterned cloak
flapping about your thin form
people streamed in every direction
in the silence and chill of an ink-blue winter night
I followed your footsteps
a light rain pitter-pattered down
misting over my eyes
and suddenly I couldn't be certain
of the true outlines
of this city and you

Imagine this city were already old
how long could we stay young?

After midnight passed
I heard another era had begun
broken beer bottles dotted the road
and the shattered glass flashed with dark green light
we paused and looked around
for the way we had come

the insubstantial wind stirred our restless hair
I kept close to you
listening to a drunkard's song disperse across the dark
   deserted alley
cheers came from the other end of the street
how should we find our way into this new century?

The journey to the century
began with a New Year's festival
bright red, brilliant and jubilant
people in ethnic dress danced
with a sleepy golden dragon while others sawed out
   squeaky tunes
on the *huqin* and others put up a white stage
and piled a symbol of unity on its cumbersome body
but that night you wore tired black clothing
had your face lost its happy expression because
you're not used to rowdiness or
you're too used to silent expression?

We walked past a public square full of people

and a pavilion newly erected on the water
the flying vermillion evoked the abstract parentheses
of history and culture
an amplified debate
blared out of the Legislative Council Building
we left the camera lights
and circled the building
not to grieve over the columns and arches about to
vanish
but because we couldn't avoid the light rain
and heavy wet air
we looked up to the roof where the goddess held her
heavenly scales
and uneasily breathed in a new century's night air
lightning burrowed into the right side of the sky
lights and singing filled the left
standing in the uncertain middle ground
I wanted to hold onto something real
you looked down at me
I turned to watch the colorful lights
in the streams of people

we were breakable as the raindrops hitting the ground

The rain started to fall harder
the street inclined and so did our drowsiness
Leaning my shoulder toward your thick eyebrows
I asked you:
when we start to get old
how long can this city stay young?

(Translated by Eleanor Goodman)

洛楓，詩人、文化評論人，香港大學文學士及哲學碩士，美國加州大學聖地牙哥校區比較文學博士，香港電台廣播節目《演藝風流》客席主持；曾任教於香港中文大學、科技大學、理工大學、演藝學院、嶺南大學等，研究範圍包括文化及電影理論、中西比較文學、性別理論、演藝及流行文化。著有詩集《距離》、《錯失》、《飛天棺材》；小説集《末代童話》、《炭燒的城》，散文集《變臉幻書》；評論集《世紀末城市：香港的流行文化》、《盛世邊緣：香港電影的性別、特技與九七政治》、《女聲喧嘩：媒介與文化閱讀》、《禁色的蝴蝶：張國榮的藝術形象》、《請勿超越黃線：香港文學的時代記認》、《情書光影：洛楓演藝評論集I》。其中詩集《飛天棺材》獲2007年第九屆香港中文文學雙年獎詩組首獎；文化評論集《禁色的蝴蝶：張國榮的藝術形象》獲「2008香港書獎」及「我最喜愛年度好書」等獎項。

Natalia S. H. Chan (penname: Lok Fung) is a poet and cultural critic. She holds a PhD in comparative literature and cultural studies from the University of California, San Diego. Her research interests include cultural and film theory, gender studies, popular culture, performance studies, cross-dressing and fashion. She is also the guest anchor of Radio Hong Kong's Performing Arts program. Her recent publications in Chinese include *Flying Coffin*, which received the 9th Biennial Award for Chinese Literature (Poetry) in 2007, and *Butterfly of Forbidden Colors: The Artistic Image of Leslie Cheung*, which received the Hong Kong Book Prize as well as the 2008 "Best Book of the Year" award.

出版 Publisher
香港中文大學出版社 The Chinese University Press

封面影像 Cover Image
北島 Bei Dao

出版日期 Date of Publication
二零一三年十一月 November 2013

國際書號 ISBN
978-962-996-625-6

香港國際詩歌之夜 2013 International Poetry Nights in Hong Kong 2013
主辦單位 Organizers
香港中文大學文學院 Faculty of Arts, The Chinese University of Hong Kong
香港浸會大學文學院 Faculty of Arts, Hong Kong Baptist University
香港科技大學人文社會科學學院 School of Humanities and Social Science, The Hong Kong University of Science and Technology

合作夥伴 In Partnership With
英國文化協會 British Council

協辦單位 Co-organizers
時刻文化 Moment Communications
香港中文大學出版社 The Chinese University Press

贊助 Sponsors
香港兆基創意書院 HKICC Lee Shau Kee School of Creativity
中國會 The China Club
周凱旋基金會 Chau Hoi Shuen Foundation

Printed in Hong Kong